PLAINSONG

Victor Tapner is an award-winning poet whose cast of characters ranges from prehistoric tribal villagers in *Flatlands*, shortlisted for the Seamus Heaney Centre Prize, to sufferers of urban conflict and artists and scientists spanning the Renaissance to the nuclear age. His poems have been shortlisted three times in the Keats-Shelley awards, and he is a recipient of the Munster Literature Centre's international chapbook prize. A freelance writer and former Financial Times journalist, he lives in Essex.

Also by Victor Tapner

Waiting to Tango (Templar Poetry, 2016)

Banquet in the Hall of Happiness (Southword Editions, 2016)

Flatlands (Salt, 2010)

Cold Rain (Grafton, 1988)

Plainsong

Victor Tapner

Broken Sleep Books

ISBN: 978-1-915760-55-5

Cover designed by Aaron Kent

Edited and Typeset by Aaron Kent

Broken Sleep Books Ltd
Rhydwen
Talgarreg
Ceredigion
SA44 4HB

Broken Sleep Books Ltd
Fair View
St Georges Road
Cornwall
PL26 7YH

Contents

Plainsong

Although reputedly illiterate, Cædmon, who tended livestock at Whitby monastery in the 7th century, is the earliest named English poet and is said to have received his calling in a dream

A rough wool blanket,
stockings of moss
my night vestments,

I sleep under beams
in this shed
on a bed of straw,

Cædmon the cowherd,
knowing only songs
from the hills:

moan of a mother
without her calf
in the early mist,

bullocks
munching grass
in the darkness.

I have no voice
in the supper hall,
no miracle tales,

no pretty poems
for the brothers' harp.
Pastures at birdcall

are heaven's music.
Christ in his kindness
lends me these words.

Spearhafoc's Flight

Spearhafoc – Old English for 'Sparrowhawk' – was an 11th century abbot and goldsmith who, after being denied consecration as Bishop of London, apparently fled with royal and church treasures, and was never seen again

In this crude dish of blackened clay
a beautiful blister of gold

teased from base alloys.
Daylight through the workshop door

wraps me in foul vapours
choking the air,

fumes from burnt flux
that solder the throat

and make one's vision dance.
I had no plan to kindle

God's grievance, only to craft
the finest ornament

worthy of my sire's crown,
and a cleric's robe woven

with threads of silver braid.
Until they stole my rightful seat.

Now they will see the jewels
of my wrath: bloodshot garnet,

rubies set in flaming filigree,
tendrils hot from the forge

that reach into their breasts
and twist a beaded wire

round their hearts.
I shall harvest their riches

and engrave my name
on their brains.

I'll show them
how a sparrowhawk

with clipped wings
flies from the devil's nest.

Time by Shadows
Nicolaus Kratzer, astronomer and clockmaker to Henry VIII

A finch on the grass
pecks a fallen apple,

ants in a hollow
strip a crippled bee,

a spider wraps a moth
too weak to leave the ground,

the orchard is fraying.
A sundial on the terrace

takes another heartbeat
from the afternoon

      shewing time by shadows,
      not only the hower of the day

      but months as they darken,
      a carved moone and starres.

Beneath a rowan tree,
watched by a nurse,

his child sleeps,
the seconds of her breath

too small to mark in stone.

This Turning World
Emery Molyneux, Elizabethan globe maker

I track the coast of Africa
and find the Spice Islands,

skirt mountains
that disfigure a continent,
ride the demons
of the seas.

This orb is fashioned
from readings I took
as we sailed the horizon

in a ship as sick
as a plague village.

Measuring the Americas
we lost souls each month,

though I'd serve again
to hear rigging creak,

catch spray over the bows

or stand on the shore
of an unknown inlet.

But one's days, too,
are unmarked on a map
and refuse to obey
any compass setting.

At my workbench
by the window
I cross an ocean

and watch the world turn
from daylight
to shadows of the room.

Pocahontas Prepares for an Audience at Court

Whenever we looked from the deck
those long weeks
the sea touched the sky on every side,
and some calm nights
as I took the air, the moon laid a path
from the stern.

Now I wake in a room
with a window of frost
whose lattice panes catch the sun
and cast a net across the matting
where I step from the bed.

Each evening my sheets
are warmed with a pan of coals
that scent the dusk
like embers of yellow pine,

velvet drapes that close me in
when the maid has gone
are heavy as deerskin,

water in a jug on the trestle
is clean enough to wash mussels.

My lady teaches me how to dress,
to walk in a farthingale,
to tuck the kirtle and carry a flounce,
to drop a curtsy

and sit without choking
in a corset stiffened with bones.
My neck is held in a cage of lace.

So many words I've learnt
since the day we sailed
that my husband says I'm ready
to suffer a speech. And yet

these hours my mind turns
head to heel, my tongue stumbles,
my hand trembles like a child's
as my lady adjusts the cuffs.

I fidget on the backstool
while she combs
the snaggles from my hair.
The oaken floor at my feet gleams
like the tidepool where I swam
with my sisters through eelgrass,
catching blue crabs and sea-stars.

And so it is each morning
when I leave my sleep
to the cry of night herons,
eagles lifting fish from the shallows,

then the call of many voices
on a day when strangers come.

Mayflower

Strands of seaweed
hang from bricks
along the harbour wall,

the bell tower
drifts with cloud
between our masts.

Grey sky, grey sea.
Such plain days
in our Dutch town

where we prayed
but lived poor,
our children schooled.

Ahead, a deep
crossing, earth
on which to kneel.

We make sail to sighs
of timbers, the squawk
of circling birds.

Age of Enlightenment

I sighed as a lover, I obeyed as a son
— Edward Gibbon

As I scrambled for my footing
amidst the ruins of the Forum
that autumn evening

I couldn't help but reflect
how Cicero and Caesar
confronted the gods

in search of omens
whenever legions left
for foreign fields.

Surveying Rome's tombs,
I held a lamp
before a sarcophagus

of blue-veined marble,
a man and woman
exchanging vows,

hands clasped,
her head loose veiled,
a bride's belt knotted

for him to untie
on their marriage bed.
When I set forth

from Oxford's cloisters
to honour the sites
of antiquity,

you became a sacrifice
on the altar
of scholarship.

Tonight,
as I put down my pen
from the last page,

I took a walk
through the gardens
and dwelt on that distant day

at the Capitol
when first I mused
on writing these histories.

I take my leave
as though of a friend
with shared memories.

The Reforms of William Wilberforce

Often I sit in the silence of the Commons
reading over my notes before prayers

while the benches are empty,
air clear, light from the high lamps

washing the floor of the chamber,
the Chaplain yet to guide with his verses:

May they never lead the nation wrongly
through love of power, desire to please,
or unworthy ideals . . .

I look for words dressed in ruffle and velvet,
for sentences that swell their waistcoats,

reasons that sneer through blackened teeth.
Sometimes I can barely find a pathway

through the scratching out, the scattered blots.
When the honourable members arrive

to take their seats, fluffing their cravats,
talking behind scented handkerchiefs,

the chamber echoes with promises
piously kept until the Chaplain rises:

But laying aside all private interests
and prejudices . . . seek to improve the condition
of all mankind . . .

Each morning I wake in the darkness
before birdsong for my devotions,

to read the Bible and Doddridge.
I've given up my place at the faro table.

The other night I saw Mrs Siddons
at Drury Lane for the last time.

The Lives of Lady Hamilton

Each way I hold the jasmine flask
the cut glass shows a different face,

stretched with hurt, pinched and mean,
now tiny like your miniature I keep

here in my dressing-box. Your hair,
I'm certain, was darker than mine,

less chestnut; your mouth, touched
with blue, a servant girl's only gift;

your skin orphan pale. That morning
when I gave you away in a shawl, I hid

my eyes, and later gave myself
as a work of art - Medea in lace,

Ariadne – a goddess modelled in oils.
I thought my other life had died.

Do you remember when you came to stay
and we walked on the lawns at Merton?

You asked if I'd always lived in a palace
and why you could never be with me.

These few phials and my silver hairbrush
are all that's left – and the letter you sent

that nestles with an admiral's breast-pin.
I've come to live in Calais now

where clouds glare down
on this forgotten street, and rain

rattles my chamber window.
These essences, I fear, are turning sour:

orange blossom more like pantry wax,
Tuscan iris sharp as tavern scent,

bottles on their tray fast drained.

On the Bridge

I.K. BRUNEL, ENGINEER, 1859
— Memorial inscription, Royal Albert Bridge, River Tamar

A hundred feet above the water
he counts the fortune
risked with every inch,

from bedrock
to painted trusses,
each stone of the towers.

Carried by couch
on a railway truck
he's surveying the site

one last time.
He has built the backbone
of a country

but can no longer walk.
The wagon stops
to let him see

the sweep of track,
an arch framing sky.
Below, the tide runs fast

against the piers;
up here, wind sharp
through the girders.

Under London

Joseph Bazalgette, Victorian civil engineer and builder of the city's sewerage network

As the lid closes
on Hammersmith Road,
muffling the crunch

of brewers' carts,
stifling shouts
from laundry windows,

he follows Mr Peters
down a manhole ladder
into the sour breath

of the weir chamber
at Counter's Creek.
Come April,

with the conduits open,
he'd be up to the top
of his boots in foul water,

but for now
the tunnels serve
as quiet caves,

the Fleet and Tyburn
funnelled
under cobbled alleys,

carrying sediments
of hillside streams
that once washed London's vales

before the Silent Highwayman
sailed down with the tide,
swathed in a fog of cholera.

Here, away from daylight,
he finds an hour's shelter
from the storms of Westminster

that have stripped
so many nights of sleep,
functionaries who say

he's draining
the nation's cash to the sea.
Through the flickering

of Mr Peters' lamp
he surveys brick arches,
a raised iron gate,

while a maze of junctions
crowd his head,
months when contours blurred

as he mapped these veins,
outflows that can take a surge
like blood to the brain,

days when he loosened
his collar to breathe,
crushed by the city's weight.

Natural Selection

Invitations were sent out, wedding dresses ordered... when almost at the last moment without the slightest warning the whole affair was broken off.
— Alfred Russel Wallace

How can I marry a man
who has eaten a bat,

who speaks of fevers
when beetles burrowed
in his ears,

ants crawling
under his eyelids,

a monstrous ape
grasping the branches
of his brain,

who believes he has seen
kangaroos climb trees,

a flying frog?

This man who thinks
he has found
the answer to life,

who paints the plumage
of a bird from heaven,

tells me of dreams
with shrunken heads

like withered fruit
hanging
over his hammock,

their faces peering
into his sleep

and now mine.

A Gap in the Field

W. G. Grace, 1848-1915; G. F. 'Fred' Grace, 1850-80

For me, that day, the wicket couldn't have been kinder
and you were never steadier,
one foot back, as Uncle had shown us,
when you took that high catch off Bonnor
right on the boundary.

The ball hugged the air so long
the bloody Aussie had turned for his third,
and everyone on the pitch
thought it would slice through your hands.

As Midwinter said,
you were the best deep field
a chap could have.

When we were boys,
practising with stones at Downend,
you could hit a sparrow from thirty yards,
though I always roasted your bowling.

One day, I remember,
I'd been at the crease in the orchard
slapping every ball you sent.
Alice and Blanche were fielding,
Edward, as usual, with his umpire's hat,
and you got so mad,
the chaffing they gave you.

I declared at lunchtime
and you held the wicket all afternoon.
You even refused
when mother called us for tea,
and we hammered on till you forced a draw
when rain stopped play.

Believe me, Fred,
runs don't come easy
when it's your waist that's padded.
The bat's straight, though,
and somewhere I'll find a gap in their cover.

You know, down at the Vauxhall end
I can still see that ball
suspended in sunlight,
almost, for a moment, challenging gravity.

Suffragettes

Emmeline Pankhurst, 1858-1928; Adela Pankhurst, 1885-1961

I taught you how to walk
in step,
your school-bag full of fireworks,

gold stars for misbehaviour.
Playground balls
became bricks through windows,

museums and galleries
closed their doors.
Our art was protest,

statues maimed,
an old master tarred.
Patience wasn't a virtue

in our house, walls hung
with newspaper cuttings,
photos of faces

trapped behind railings,
truncheons ready to strike.
We were a family

handcuffed by headlines.
In reeking cells
we starved for the right

to put a cross in a box,
watching our friends
force fed

or gagged with threats.
What a clever girl you were
to flee the field

when the guns were primed,
watching the battle
from your hilltop.

I gave you a traitor's ticket
and stood at the quayside
to see you off,

but when you waved from the rail
our goodbyes were drowned
in the noise of the crowd.

Acknowledgements

Some of these poems first appeared thanks to *Ambit, Iota, The London Magazine, The New Writer, Poetry London,* the Charles Causley Trust and the Keats-Shelley Memorial Association.

'The Reforms of William Wilberforce' was shortlisted for the Keats-Shelley Poetry Prize; 'Under London' was commended in the Poetry London Clore Prize; 'A Gap in the Field' was highly commended in the Charles Causley International Poetry Competition; and 'Pocahontas Prepares for an Audience at Court' was part of a grouping that won The New Writer Poetry Collection Prize.

LAY OUT YOUR UNREST

Milton Keynes UK
Ingram Content Group UK Ltd.
UKHW012023081223
434013UK00004B/112